D0969530

Selected Poems
1968–1986

Also by Paul Muldoon

New Weather (1973)
Mules (1977)
Why Brownlee Left (1980)
Quoof (1983)
Meeting the British (1987)
Madoc: A Mystery (1990)

The Faber Book of Contemporary Irish Poetry
(editor) (1986)

Paul Muldoon

SELECTED

POEMS

1968–1986

The Noonday Press

Farrar, Straus and Giroux

New York

Copyright © Paul Muldoon 1973, 1977, 1980,
1983, 1986, 1987
All rights reserved
Hardcover edition published in 1987 by The Ecco Press
First Noonday Press edition, 1993
Printed in the United States of America

Library of Congress Cataloging-in-Publication Data
Muldoon, Paul.
Selected poems, 1968–1986.
I. Title.
PR6063.U367A6   1987   821'.914   87-6752

Contents

from New Weather

from Mules

from Why Brownlee Left

from Quoof

from Meeting the British

from
NEW WEATHER

Wind and Tree

In the way that most of the wind
Happens where there are trees,

Most of the world is centred
About ourselves.

Often where the wind has gathered
The trees together,

One tree will take
Another in her arms and hold.

Their branches that are grinding
Madly together,

It is no real fire.
They are breaking each other.

Often I think I should be like
The single tree, going nowhere,

Since my own arm could not and would not
Break the other. Yet by my broken bones

I tell new weather.

Dancers at the Moy

This Italian square
And circling plain
Black once with mares
And their stallions,
The flat Blackwater
Turning its stones

Over hour after hour
As their hooves shone
And lifted together
Under the black rain,
One or other Greek war
Now coloured the town

Blacker than ever before
With hungry stallions
And their hungry mares
Like hammocks of skin,
The flat Blackwater
Unable to contain

Itself as horses poured
Over acres of grain
In a black and gold river.
No band of Athenians
Arrived at the Moy fair
To buy for their campaign,

Peace having been declared
And a treaty signed.
The black and gold river
Ended as a trickle of brown
Where those horses tore
At briars and whins,

Ate the flesh of each other
Like people in famine.
The flat Blackwater
Hobbled on its stones
With a wild stagger
And sag in its backbone,

The local people gathered
The white skeletons.
Horses buried for years
Under the foundations
Give their earthen floors
The ease of trampolines.

The Waking Father

My father and I are catching spricklies
Out of the Oona river.
They have us feeling righteous,
The way we have thrown them back.
Our benevolence is astounding.

When my father stood out in the shallows
It occurred to me
The spricklies might have been piranhas,
The river a red carpet
Rolling out from where he had just stood,

Or I wonder now if he is dead or sleeping.
For if he is dead I would have his grave
Secret and safe;
I would turn the river out of its course,
Lay him in its bed, bring it round again.

No one would question
That he had treasures or his being a king,
Telling now of the real fish farther down.

Thrush

I guessed the letter
    Must be yours. I recognized
The cuttle ink,
    The serif on
The P. I read the postmark and the date,
    Impatience held
By a paperweight.
    I took your letter at eleven
To the garden
    With my tea.
And suddenly the yellow gum secreted
    Halfwayup
The damson bush
    Had grown a shell.
I let those scentless pages fall
    And took it
In my feckless hand. I turned it over
    On its back
To watch your mouth
    Withdraw. Making a lean, white fist
Out of my freckled hand.

Hedgehog

The snail moves like a
Hovercraft, held up by a
Rubber cushion of itself,
Sharing its secret

With the hedgehog. The hedgehog
Shares its secret with no one.
We say, *Hedgehog, come out
Of yourself and we will love you.*

*We mean no harm. We want
Only to listen to what
You have to say. We want
Your answers to our questions.*

The hedgehog gives nothing
Away, keeping itself to itself.
We wonder what a hedgehog
Has to hide, why it so distrusts.

We forget the god
Under this crown of thorns.
We forget that never again
Will a god trust in the world.

Good Friday, 1971. Driving Westward

It was good going along with the sun
Through Ballygawley, Omagh and Strabane.
I started out as it was getting light
And caught sight of hares all along the road
That looked to have been taking a last fling,
Doves making the most of their offerings
As if all might not be right with the day

Where I moved through morning towards the sea.
I was glad that I would not be alone.
Those children who travel badly as wine
Waved as they passed in their uppity cars
And now the first cows were leaving the byres,
The first lorry had delivered its load.
A whole country was fresh after the night

Though people were still fighting for the last
Dreams and changing their faces where I paused
To read the first edition of the truth.
I gave a lift to the girl out of love
And crossed the last great frontier at Lifford.
An iffing and butting herd
Of goats. Letterkenny had just then laid

Open its heart and we passed as new blood
Back into the grey flesh of Donegal.
The sky went out of its way for the hills
And life was changing down for the sharp bends
Where the road had put its thin brown arm round
A hill and held on tight out of pure fear.
Errigal stepped out suddenly in our

Path and the thin arm tightened round the waist
Of the mountain and for a time I lost
Control and she thought we had hit something big
But I had seen nothing, perhaps a stick
Lying across the road. I glanced back once
And there was nothing but a heap of stones.
We had just dropped in from nowhere for lunch

In Gaoth Dobhair, I happy and she convinced
Of the death of more than lamb or herring.
She stood up there and then, face full of drink,
And announced that she and I were to blame
For something killed along the way we came.
Children were warned that it was rude to stare,
Left with their parents for a breath of air.

The Cure for Warts

Had I been the seventh son of a seventh son
Living at the dead centre of a wood
Or at the dead end of a lane,
I might have cured by my touch alone
That pair of warts nippling your throat,

Who had no faith in a snail rubbed on your skin
And spiked on a thorn like a king's head,
In my spittle on shrunken stone,
In bathing yourself at the break of dawn
In dew or the black cock's or the bull's blood,

In other such secrets told by way of a sign
Of the existence of one or other god,
So I doubt if any woman's son
Could have cured by his touch alone
That pair of warts nibbling your throat.

Identities

When I reached the sea
I fell in with another who had just come
From the interior. Her family
Had figured in a past regime
But her father was now imprisoned.

She had travelled, only by night,
Escaping just as her own warrant
Arrived and stealing the police boat,
As far as this determined coast.

As it happened, we were staying at the same
Hotel, pink and goodish for the tourist
Quarter. She came that evening to my room
Asking me to go to the capital,
Offering me wristwatch and wallet,
To search out an old friend who would steal
Papers for herself and me. Then to be married,
We could leave from that very harbour.

I have been wandering since, back up the streams
That had once flowed simply one into the other,
One taking the other's name.

Elizabeth

The birds begin as an isolated shower
Over the next county, their slow waltz
Swerving as if to avoid something
Every so often, getting thin
As it slants, making straight for
Us over your father's darkening fields,
Till their barely visible wings
Remember themselves, they are climbing again.
We wonder what could bring them so far

Inland, they belong to the sea.
You hold on hard like holding on to life,
Following the flock as it bends
And collapses like a breeze.
You want to know where from and why,
Though birds would never keep still long enough
For me to be able to take a count.
We'll hold our ground and they'll pass.
But they're coming right overhead, you cry,

And storm inside and bang the door.
All I can hear is the flicking of bolts.
The one dull window is shutting
Its eye as if a wayward hurricane
With the name of a girl and the roar
Of devils were beginning its assaults.
But these are the birds of a child's painting,
Filling the page till nothing else is seen.
You are inside yet, pacing the floor,

Having been trapped in every way.
You hold yourself as your own captive;
My promised children are in your hands,
Hostaged by you in your father's old house.
I call you now for all the names of the day,
Lizzie and Liz and plain Beth.
You do not make the slightest sound.
When you decide that you have nothing to lose
And come out, there is nothing you can say;

We watch them hurtle, a recklessness of stars,
Into the acre that has not cooled
From my daylong ploughings and harrowings,
Their greys flecking the brown,
Till one, and then two, and now four
Sway back across your father's patchwork quilt,
Into your favourite elm. They will stay long
Enough to underline how soon they will be gone,
As you seem thinner than you were before.

The Field Hospital

Taking, giving back their lives
By the strength of our bare hands,
By the silence of our knives,
We answer to no grey South

Nor blue North. Not self defence,
The lie of just wars, neither
Cold nor hot blood's difference
In their discharging of guns,

But that hillside of fresh graves.
Would this girl brought to our tents
From whose flesh we have removed
Shot that George, on his day off,

Will use to weight fishing lines,
Who died screaming for ether,
Yet protest our innocence?
George lit the lanterns, in danced

Those gigantic, yellow moths
That brushed right over her wounds,
Pinning themselves to our sleeves
Like medals given the brave.

from
MULES

Lunch with Pancho Villa

I

'Is it really a revolution, though?'
I reached across the wicker table
With another $10,000 question.
My celebrated pamphleteer,
Co-author of such volumes
As *Blood on the Rose*,
The Dream and the Drums,
And *How It Happened Here*,
Would pour some untroubled Muscatel
And settle back in his cane chair.

'Look, son. Just look around you.
People are getting themselves killed
Left, right and centre
While you do what? Write rondeaux?
There's more to living in this country
Than stars and horses, pigs and trees,
Not that you'd guess it from your poems.
Do you never listen to the news?
You want to get down to something true,
Something a little nearer home.'

I called again later that afternoon,
A quiet suburban street.
'You want to stand back a little
When the world's at your feet.'
I'd have liked to have heard some more
Of his famous revolution.

I rang the bell, and knocked hard
On what I remembered as his front door,
That opened then, as such doors do,
Directly on to a back yard.

II

Not any back yard, I'm bound to say,
And not a thousand miles away
From here. No one's taken in, I'm sure,
By such a mild invention.
But where (I wonder myself) do I stand,
In relation to a table and chair,
The quince-tree I forgot to mention,
That suburban street, the door, the yard –
All made up as I went along
As things that people live among.

And such a person as lived there!
My celebrated pamphleteer!
Of course, I gave it all away
With those preposterous titles.
The Bloody Rose? The Dream and the Drums?
The three-day-wonder of the flowering plum!
Or was I desperately wishing
To have been their other co-author.
Or, at least, to own a first edition
Of *The Boot Boys and Other Battles?*

'When are you going to tell the truth?'
For there's no such book, so far as I know,
As *How it Happened Here*,
Though there may be. There may.

What should I say to this callow youth
Who learned to write last winter –
One of those correspondence courses –
And who's coming to lunch today?
He'll be rambling on, no doubt,
About pigs and trees, stars and horses.

The Big House

I was only the girl under the stairs
But I was the first to notice something was wrong.
I was always first up and about, of course.
Those hens would never lay two days running
In the same place. I would rise early
And try round the haggard for fresh nests.
The mistress let me keep the egg-money.

And that particular night there were guests,
Mrs de Groot from the bridge set
And a young man who wrote stories for children,
So I wanted everything to be just right
When they trooped down to breakfast that morning.

I slept at the very top of that rambling house,
A tiny room with only a sky-light window.
I had brushed my hair and straightened my dress
And was just stepping into the corridor
When it struck me. That old boarded-up door
Was flung open. A pile of rubble and half-bricks
Was strewn across the landing floor.

I went on down. I was stooping among the hay-stacks
When there came a clatter of hooves in the yard.
The squire's sure-footed little piebald mare
Had found her own way home, as always.
He swayed some. Then fell headlong on the cobbles.

22

There was not so much as the smell of whiskey on him.
People still hold he had died of fright,
That the house was haunted by an elder brother
Who was murdered for his birthright.
People will always put two and two together.

What I remember most of that particular morning
Was how calmly everyone took the thing.
The mistress insisted that life would go on quietly
As it always had done. Breakfast was served
At nine exactly. I can still hear Mrs de Groot
Telling how she had once bid seven hearts.
The young man's stories were for grown-ups, really.

Cass and Me

Do you remember me, Cass,
The brim of his hat over my face,
My father's slicker trailing the ground
When I was a child? Once you came round

And I climbed on your shoulders.
Once you were stronger, taller, older.
We leaned out across the yard
As a giant would across the world.

The sow fled West with her farrow,
The hound made a rainbow under the barrow,
The cock crowed out of time,

So large we loomed.
Which of us, I wonder, had grown.
Whose were those wide eyes at my groin?

Ned Skinner

Was 'a barbaric yawp',
If you took Aunt Sarah at her word.
He would step over the mountain
Of a summer afternoon
To dress a litter of pigs
On my uncle's farm.

Aunt Sarah would keep me in,
Taking me on her lap
Till it was over.
Ned Skinner wiped his knife
And rinsed his hands
In the barrel at the door-step.

He winked, and gripped my arm.
'It doesn't hurt, not so's you'd notice,
And God never slams one door
But another's lying open.
Them same pigs can see the wind.'
My uncle had given him five shillings.

Ned Skinner came back
While my uncle was in the fields.
'Sarah,' he was calling, 'Sarah.
You weren't so shy in our young day.
You remember yon time in Archer's loft?'
His face blazed at the scullery window.
'Remember? When the hay was won.'

Aunt Sarah had the door on the snib.
'That's no kind of talk
To be coming over. Now go you home.'
Silence. Then a wheeze.
We heard the whiskey-jug
Tinkle, his boots diminish in the yard.
Aunt Sarah put on a fresh apron.

Ma

Old photographs would have her bookish, sitting
Under a willow. I take that to be a croquet-
Lawn. She reads aloud, no doubt from Rupert Brooke.
The month is always May or June.

Or with the stranger on the motor-bike.
Not my father, no. This one's all crew-cut
And polished brass buttons.
An American soldier, perhaps.

               And the full moon
Swaying over Keenaghan, the orchards and the cannery,
Thins to a last yellow-hammer, and goes.
The neighbours gather, all Keenaghan and Collegelands,
There is story-telling. Old miners at Coalisland
Going into the ground. Swinging, for fear of the gas,
The soft flame of a canary.

Our Lady of Ardboe

I

Just there, in a corner of the whin-field,
Just where the thistles bloom.
She stood there as in Bethlehem
One night in nineteen fifty-three or four.

The girl leaning over the half-door
Saw the cattle kneel, and herself knelt.

II

I suppose that a farmer's youngest daughter
Might, as well as the next, unravel
The winding road to Christ's navel.

Who's to know what's knowable?
Milk from the Virgin Mother's breast,
A feather off the Holy Ghost?
The fairy thorn? The holy well?

Our simple wish for there being more to life
Than a job, a car, a house, a wife –
The fixity of running water.

For I like to think, as I step these acres,
That a holy well is no more shallow
Nor plummetless than the pools of Shiloh,
The fairy thorn no less true than the Cross.

III

Mother of our Creator, Mother of our Saviour,
Mother most amiable, Mother most admirable.
Virgin most prudent, Virgin most venerable,
Mother inviolate, Mother undefiled.

And I walk waist-deep among purples and golds
With one arm as long as the other.

Blemish

Were it indeed an accident of birth
That she looks on the gentle earth
And the seemingly gentle sky
Through one brown, and one blue eye.

The Bearded Woman, by Ribera

I've seen one in a fairground,
Swigging a quart of whiskey,
But nothing like this lady
Who squats in the foreground
To suckle the baby,
With what must be her husband
Almost out of the picture.

Might this be the Holy Family
Gone wrong?

Her face belongs to my grand-da
Except that her beard
Is so luxuriantly black.
One pap, her right, is bared
And borrowed by her child,
Who could not be less childlike.
He's ninety, too, if he's a day.

I'm taken completely
By this so unlikely Madonna.

Yet my eye is drawn once again,
Almost against its wishes,
To the figure in the shadows,
Willowy, and clean-shaven,
As if he has simply wandered in
Between mending that fuse
And washing the breakfast dishes.

The Mixed Marriage

My father was a servant-boy.
When he left school at ten or eleven
He took up billhook and loy
To win the ground he would never own.

My mother was the school-mistress,
The world of Castor and Pollux.
There were twins in her own class.
She could never tell which was which.

She had read one volume of Proust,
He knew the cure for farcy.
I flitted between a hold in the hedge
And a room in the Latin Quarter.

When she had cleared the supper-table
She opened *The Acts of the Apostles*,
Aesop's Fables, *Gulliver's Travels*.
Then my mother went on upstairs

And my father further dimmed the light
To get back to hunting with ferrets
Or the factions of the faction-fights –
The Ribbon Boys, the Caravats.

Duffy's Circus

Once Duffy's Circus had shaken out its tent
In the big field near the Moy
God may as well have left Ireland
And gone up a tree. My father had said so.

There was no such thing as the five-legged calf,
The God of Creation
Was the God of Love.
My father chose to share such Nuts of Wisdom.

Yet across the Alps of each other the elephants
Trooped. Nor did it matter
When Wild Bill's Rain Dance
Fell flat. Some clown emptied a bucket of stars

Over the swankiest part of the crowd.
I had lost my father in the rush and slipped
Out the back. Now I heard
For the first time that long-drawn-out cry.

It came from somewhere beyond the corral.
A dwarf on stilts. Another dwarf.
I sidled past some trucks. From under a freighter
I watched a man sawing a woman in half.

Mules

Should they not have the best of both worlds?

Her feet of clay gave the lie
To the star burned in our mare's brow.
Would Parsons' jackass not rest more assured
That cross wrenched from his shoulders?

We had loosed them into one field.
I watched Sam Parsons and my quick father
Tense for the punch below their belts,
For what was neither one thing or the other.

It was as though they had shuddered
To think, of their gaunt, sexless foal
Dropped tonight in the cowshed.

We might yet claim that it sprang from earth
Were it not for the afterbirth
Trailed like some fine, silk parachute,
That we would know from what heights it fell.

Armageddon, Armageddon

I

At last, someone had heard tell of Larry Durrell.
We leaned round headland after headland
When there it was, his Snow-White Villa.
Wasn't it dazzling?
                    Well, it was rather white.
The orange and lemon groves, the olives,
Are wicked for this purity of light.
In a while now we will go ashore, to Mouse Island.

The light is failing. Our mouths are numb with aniseed,
Her little breasts are sour as Jeanne Duval's.
And darknesses weigh down further the burgeoning trees
Where she kneels in her skimpy dress
To gather armful after armful.
Nuzzling the deep blues, the purples. Spitting the stars.

II

When Oisin came back to Ireland
After three hundred years
On one of those enchanted islands
Somewhere in the Western Seas,

He thought nothing of dismounting
From his enchanted steed
To be one again with the mountains,
The bogs and the little fields.

There and then he began to stoop,
His hair, and all his teeth, fell out,
A mildewed belt, a rusted buckle.
The clays were heavy, black or yellow,
Those were the colours of his boots.
And I know something of how he felt.

III

Not to worry. From where I lived
We might watch Long Bullets being played,
Follow the course of a pair of whippets,
Try to keep in time with a Lambeg Drum.

There'd be Derryscollop, and Cloveneden,
The parish where W. R. Rodgers held sway.
And where the first Orange Lodge was founded,
An orchard full of No Surrenders.

We could always go closer if you wanted,
To where Macha had challenged the charioteer
And Swift the Houyhnhnm,
An open field where the twins were whelped.
Then, the scene of the Armagh Rail Disaster.
Why not brave the Planetarium?

IV

You had been sleeping, O my lover,
A good half-hour, it seemed,
And I woke you only to discover
How you might have dreamed,
How you might have dreamed.

Might some glistening inspector
By his one dull incisor
And simple rule-of-thumb
Already have beavered through
To our last-carriage-but-one?

Did he hint something of blockades,
Of trees felled across the lines,
And then hand back our tickets
Ratified by a constellation?

V

Now that I had some idea of our whereabouts
We could slow a little and not be afraid.
Who was that? Only the bull behind the hedge,
It was showing us the whites of its eyes.

Why should those women be carrying water
If all the wells were poisoned, as they said,
And the fish littering the river?
Had the sheep been divided from the goats,
Were Twin and Twin at each other's throats?

I knew these fields. How long were they fallow?
Those had been Archer's sixty yellow acres,
These Hunter's forty green and grey.
Had Hunter and Archer got it into their heads
That they would take the stars in their strides?

VI

My brother had mislaid his voice
Since it happened. His eyes had grown simple,
His hand alone would describe
Our father's return from the betting shop
To be torn between his own two ponies,
Their going their different ways.

He had guarded our mother bent-double
Over the kitchen sink, her face in the basin.
She had broken another of her best dishes,
We would bury her when we were able.

Some violence had been done to Grace,
She had left for our next-of-kin.
My brother gave us half of his last mangold
And the warning of bayonets fixed in the bushes.

VII

A summer night in Keenaghan
So dark my light had lingered near its lamp
For fear of it. Nor was I less afraid.
At the Mustard Seed Mission all was darkness.

I had gone out with the kettle
To a little stream that lay down in itself
And breathed through a hollow reed
When yon black beetle lighted on my thumb
And tickled along my palm
Like a blood-blister with a mind of its own.

My hand might well have been some flat stone
The way it made for the underside.
I had to turn my wrist against its wont
To have it walk in the paths of uprightness.

from

WHY BROWNLEE LEFT

The Weepies

Most Saturday afternoons
At the local Hippodrome
Saw the Pathe-News rooster,
Then the recurring dream

Of a lonesome drifter
Through uninterrupted range.
Will Hunter, so gifted
He could peel an orange

In a single, fluent gesture,
Was the leader of our gang.
The curtain rose this afternoon
On a lion, not a gong.

When the crippled girl
Who wanted to be a dancer
Met the married man
Who was dying of cancer,

Our hankies unfurled
Like flags of surrender.
I believe something fell asunder
In even Will Hunter's hands.

Bran

While he looks into the eyes of women
Who have let themselves go,
While they sigh and they moan
For pure joy,

He weeps for the boy on that small farm
Who takes an oatmeal Labrador
In his arms,
Who knows all there is of rapture.

Cuba

My eldest sister arrived home that morning
In her white muslin evening dress.
'Who the hell do you think you are,
Running out to dances in next to nothing?
As though we hadn't enough bother
With the world at war, if not at an end.'
My father was pounding the breakfast-table.

'Those Yankees were touch and go as it was –
If you'd heard Patton in Armagh –
But this Kennedy's nearly an Irishman
So he's not much better than ourselves.
And him with only to say the word.
If you've got anything on your mind
Maybe you should make your peace with God.'

I could hear May from beyond the curtain.
'Bless me, Father, for I have sinned.
I told a lie once, I was disobedient once.
And, Father, a boy touched me once.'
'Tell me, child. Was this touch immodest?
Did he touch your breast, for example?'
'He brushed against me, Father. Very gently.'

The Boundary Commission

You remember that village where the border ran
Down the middle of the street,
With the butcher and baker in different states?
Today he remarked how a shower of rain

Had stopped so cleanly across Golightly's lane
It might have been a wall of glass
That had toppled over. He stood there, for ages,
To wonder which side, if any, he should be on.

Anseo

When the Master was calling the roll
At the primary school in Collegelands,
You were meant to call back *Anseo*
And raise your hand
As your name occurred.
Anseo, meaning here, here and now,
All present and correct,
Was the first word of Irish I spoke.
The last name on the ledger
Belonged to Joseph Mary Plunkett Ward
And was followed, as often as not,
By silence, knowing looks,
A nod and a wink, the Master's droll
'And where's our little Ward-of-court?'

I remember the first time he came back
The Master had sent him out
Along the hedges
To weigh up for himself and cut
A stick with which he would be beaten.
After a while, nothing was spoken;
He would arrive as a matter of course
With an ash-plant, a salley-rod.
Or, finally, the hazel-wand
He had whittled down to a whip-lash,
Its twist of red and yellow lacquers
Sanded and polished,
And altogether so delicately wrought
That he had engraved his initials on it.

I last met Joseph Mary Plunkett Ward
In a pub just over the Irish border.
He was living in the open,
In a secret camp
On the other side of the mountain.
He was fighting for Ireland,
Making things happen.
And he told me, Joe Ward,
Of how he had risen through the ranks
To Quartermaster, Commandant:
How every morning at parade
His volunteers would call back *Anseo*
And raise their hands
As their names occurred.

Why Brownlee Left

Why Brownlee left, and where he went,
Is a mystery even now.
For if a man should have been content
It was him; two acres of barley,
One of potatoes, four bullocks,
A milker, a slated farmhouse.
He was last seen going out to plough
On a March morning, bright and early.

By noon Brownlee was famous;
They had found all abandoned, with
The last rig unbroken, his pair of black
Horses, like man and wife,
Shifting their weight from foot to
Foot, and gazing into the future.

Immrama

I, too, have trailed my father's spirit
From the mud-walled cabin behind the mountain
Where he was born and bred,
TB and scarlatina,
The farm where he was first hired out,
To Wigan, to Crewe junction,
A building-site from which he disappeared
And took passage, almost, for Argentina.

The mountain is coming down with hazel,
The building-site a slum,
While he has gone no further than Brazil.

That's him on the verandah, drinking rum
With a man who might be a Nazi,
His children asleep under their mosquito-nets.

Promises, Promises

I am stretched out under the lean-to
Of an old tobacco-shed
On a farm in North Carolina.
A cardinal sings from the dogwood
For the love of marijuana.
His song goes over my head.
There is such splendour in the grass
I might be the picture of happiness.
Yet I am utterly bereft
Of the low hills, the open-ended sky,
The wave upon wave of pasture
Rolling in, and just as surely
Falling short of my bare feet.
Whatever is passing is passing me by.

I am with Raleigh, near the Atlantic,
Where we have built a stockade
Around our little colony.
Give him his scallop-shell of quiet,
His staff of faith to walk upon,
His scrip of joy, immortal diet –
We are some eighty souls
On whom Raleigh will hoist his sails.
He will return, years afterwards,
To wonder where and why
We might have altogether disappeared,
Only to glimpse us here and there
As one fair strand in her braid,
The blue in an Indian girl's dead eye.

I am stretched out under the lean-to
Of an old tobacco-shed
On a farm in North Carolina,
When someone or other, warm, naked,
Stirs within my own skeleton
And stands on tip-toe to look out
Over the horizon,
Through the zones, across the ocean.
The cardinal sings from a redbud
For the love of one slender and shy,
The flight after flight of stairs
To her room in Bayswater,
The damson freckle on her throat
That I kissed when we kissed Goodbye.

Truce

It begins with one or two soldiers
And one or two following
With hampers over their shoulders.
They might be off wildfowling

As they would another Christmas Day,
So gingerly they pick their steps.
No one seems sure of what to do.
All stop when one stops.

A fire gets lit. Some spread
Their greatcoats on the frozen ground.
Polish vodka, fruit and bread
Are broken out and passed round.

The air of an old German song,
The rules of Patience, are the secrets
They'll share before long.
They draw on their last cigarettes

As Friday-night lovers, when it's over,
Might get up from their mattresses
To congratulate each other
And exchange names and addresses.

Holy Thursday

They're kindly here, to let us linger so late,
Long after the shutters are up.
A waiter glides from the kitchen with a plate
Of stew, or some thick soup,

And settles himself at the next table but one.
We know, you and I, that it's over,
That something or other has come between
Us, whatever we are, or were.

The waiter swabs his plate with bread
And drains what's left of his wine,
Then rearranges, one by one,
The knife, the fork, the spoon, the napkin,
The table itself, the chair he's simply borrowed,
And smiles, and bows to his own absence.

Making the Move

When Ulysses braved the wine-dark sea
He left his bow with Penelope,

Who would bend for no one but himself.
I edge along the book-shelf,

Past bad Lord Byron, Raymond Chandler,
Howard Hughes; The Hidden Years,

Past Blaise Pascal, who, bound in hide,
Divined the void to his left side:

Such books as one may think one owns
Unloose themselves like stones

And clatter down into this wider gulf
Between myself and my good wife;

A primus stove, a sleeping-bag,
The bow I bought through a catalogue

When I was thirteen or fourteen
That would bend, and break, for anyone,

Its boyish length of maple upon maple
Unseasoned and unsupple.

Were I embarking on that wine-dark sea
I would bring my bow along with me.

Immram

I was fairly and squarely behind the eight
That morning in Foster's pool-hall
When it came to me out of the blue
In the shape of a sixteen-ounce billiard cue
That lent what he said some little weight.
'Your old man was an ass-hole.
That makes an ass-hole out of you.'
My grand-father hailed from New York State.
My grand-mother was part Cree.
This must be some new strain in my pedigree.

The billiard-player had been big, and black,
Dressed to kill, or inflict a wound,
And had hung around the pin-table
As long as it took to smoke a panatella.
I was clinging to an ice-pack
On which the Titanic might have foundered
When I was suddenly bedazzled
By a little silver knick-knack
That must have fallen from his hat-band.
I am telling this exactly as it happened.

I suppose that I should have called the cops
Or called it a day and gone home
And done myself, and you, a favour.
But I wanted to know more about my father.
So I drove west to Paradise
Where I was greeted by the distant hum
Of *Shall We Gather at the River?*
The perfect introduction to the kind of place
Where people go to end their lives.
It might have been *Bringing In the Sheaves.*

My mother had just been fed by force,
A pint of lukewarm water through a rubber hose.
I hadn't seen her in six months or a year,
Not since my father had disappeared.
Now she'd taken an overdose
Of alcohol and barbiturates,
And this, I learned, was her third.
I was told then by a male nurse
That if I came back at the end of the week
She might be able to bring herself to speak.

Which brought me round to the Atlantic Club.
The Atlantic Club was an old grain-silo
That gave on to the wharf.
Not the kind of place you took your wife
Unless she had it in mind to strip
Or you had a mind to put her up for sale.
I knew how my father had come here by himself
And maybe thrown a little crap
And watched his check double, and treble,
With highball hard on the heels of highball.

She was wearing what looked like a dead fox
Over a low-cut sequinned gown,
And went by the name of Susan, or Suzanne.
A girl who would never pass out of fashion
So long as there's an 'if' in California.
I stood her one or two pink gins
And the talk might have come round to passion
Had it not been for a pair of thugs
Who suggested that we both take a wander,
She upstairs, I into the wild, blue yonder.

They came bearing down on me out of nowhere.
A Buick and a Chevrolet.
They were heading towards a grand slam.
Salami on rye. I was the salami.
So much for my faith in human nature.
The age of chivalry how are you?
But I side-stepped them, neatly as Salome,
So they came up against one another
In a moment of intense heat and light,
Like a couple of turtles on their wedding-night.

Both were dead. Of that I was almost certain.
When I looked into their eyes
I sensed the import of their recent visions,
How you must get all of wisdom
As you pass through a wind-shield.
One's frizzled hair was dyed
A peroxide blond, his sinewy arms emblazoned
With tattoos, his vest marked *Urgent*.
All this was taking on a shape
That might be clearer after a night's sleep.

When the only thing I had ever held in common
With anyone else in the world
Was the ramshackle house on Central Boulevard
That I shared with my child-bride
Until she dropped out to join a commune,
You can imagine how little I was troubled
To kiss Goodbye to its weathered clapboard.
When I nudged the rocker on the porch
It rocked as though it might never rest.
It seemed that I would forever be driving west.

I was in luck. She'd woken from her slumbers
And was sitting out among flowering shrubs.
All might have been peace and harmony
In that land of milk and honey
But for the fact that our days are numbered,
But for Foster's, the Atlantic Club,
And now that my father owed Redpath money.
Redpath. She told me how his empire
Ran a little more than half-way to Hell
But began on the top floor of the Park Hotel.

Steel and glass were held in creative tension
That afternoon in the Park.
I strode through the cavernous lobby
And found myself behind a nervous couple
Who registered as Mr and Mrs Alfred Tennyson.
The unsmiling, balding desk-clerk
Looked like a man who would sell an alibi
To King Kong on the Empire State building,
So I thought better of passing the time of day.
I took the elevator all the way.

You remember how, in a half-remembered dream,
You found yourself in a long corridor,
How behind the first door there was nothing,
Nothing behind the second,
Then how you swayed from room to empty room
Until, beyond that last half-open door
You heard a telephone . . . and you were wakened
By a woman's voice asking you to come
To the Atlantic Club, between six and seven,
And when you came, to come alone.

I was met, not by the face behind the voice,
But by yet another aide-de-camp
Who would have passed for a Barbary pirate
With a line in small-talk like a parrot
And who ferried me past an outer office
To a not ungracious inner sanctum.
I did a breast-stroke through the carpet,
Went under once, only to surface
Alongside the raft of a banquet-table –
A whole roast pig, its mouth fixed on an apple.

Beyond the wall-length, two-way mirror
There was still more to feast your eyes upon
As Susan, or Susannah, danced
Before what looked like an invited audience,
A select band of admirers
To whom she would lay herself open.
I was staring into the middle distance
Where two men and a dog were mowing her meadow
When I was hit by a hypodermic syringe.
And I entered a world equally rich and strange.

There was one who can only have been asleep
Among row upon row of sheeted cadavers
In what might have been the Morgue
Of all the cities of America,
Who beckoned me towards her slab
And silently drew back the covers
On the vermilion omega
Where she had been repeatedly stabbed,
Whom I would carry over the threshold of pain
That she might come and come and come again.

I came to, under a steaming pile of trash
In the narrow alley-way
Behind that old Deep Water Baptist mission
Near the corner of Sixteenth and Ocean –
A blue-eyed boy, the Word made flesh
Amid no hosannahs nor hallelujahs
But the strains of Blind Lemon Jefferson
That leaked from the church
Through a hole in a tiny, stained-glass window,
In what was now a torrent, now had dwindled.

And honking to Blind Lemon's blues guitar
Was a solitary, black cat
Who would have turned the heads of Harlem.
He was no louder than a fire-alarm,
A full-length coat of alligator,
An ermine stole, his wide-brimmed hat
Festooned with family heirlooms.
I watch him trickle a fine, white powder
Into his palm, so not a grain would spill,
Then snort it through a rolled-up dollar bill.

This was angel dust, dust from an angel's wing
Where it glanced off the land of cocaine,
Be that Bolivia, Peru.
Or snow from the slopes of the Andes, so pure
It would never melt in spring.
But you know how over every Caliban
There's Ariel, and behind him, Prospero;
Everyone taking a cut, dividing and conquering
With lactose and dextrose,
Everyone getting right up everyone else's nose.

I would tip-toe round by the side of the church
For a better view. Some fresh cement.
I trod as lightly there
As a mere mortal at Grauman's Chinese Theatre.
An oxy-acetylene torch.
There were two false-bottomed
Station-wagons. I watched Mr See-You-Later
Unload a dozen polythene packs
From one to the other. *The Urgent Shipping Company.*
It behoved me to talk to the local P.D.

'My father, God rest him, he held this theory
That the Irish, the American Irish,
Were really the thirteenth tribe,
The Israelites of Europe.
All along, my father believed in fairies
But he might as well have been Jewish.'
His laugh was a slight hiccup.
I guessed that Lieutenant Brendan O'Leary's
Grand-mother's pee was green,
And that was why she had to leave old Skibbereen.

Now, what was all this about the Atlantic cabaret,
Urgent, the top floor of the Park?
When had I taken it into my head
That somebody somewhere wanted to see me dead?
Who? No, Redpath was strictly on the level.
So why, rather than drag in the Narcs.,
Why didn't he and I drive over to Ocean Boulevard
At Eighteenth Street, or wherever?
Would I mind stepping outside while he made a call
To such-and-such a luminary at City Hall?

We counted thirty-odd of those brown-eyed girls
Who ought to be in pictures,
Bronzed, bleached, bare-breasted,
Bare-assed to a man,
All sitting, cross-legged, in a circle
At the feet of this life-guard out of Big Sur
Who made an exhibition
Of his dorsals and his pectorals
While one by one his disciples took up the chant
The Lord is my surf-board. I shall not want.

He went on to explain to O'Leary and myself
How only that morning he had acquired the lease
On the old Baptist mission,
Though his was a wholly new religion.
He called it *The Way Of The One Wave.*
This one wave was sky-high, like a wall of glass,
And had come to him in a vision.
You could ride it forever, effortlessly.
The Lieutenant was squatting before his new guru.
I would inform the Missing Persons Bureau.

His name? I already told you his name.
Forty-nine. Fifty come July.
Five ten or eleven. One hundred and eighty pounds.
He could be almost anyone.
And only now was it brought home to me
How rarely I looked in his eyes,
Which were hazel. His hair was mahogany brown.
There was a scar on his left forearm
From that time he got himself caught in the works
Of a saw-mill near Ithaca, New York.

65

I was just about getting things into perspective
When a mile-long white Cadillac
Came sweeping out of the distant past
Like a wayward Bay mist,
A transport of joy. There was that chauffeur
From the 1931 Sears Roebuck catalogue,
Susannah, as you guessed,
And this refugee from F. Scott Fitzgerald
Who looked as if he might indeed own the world.
His name was James Earl Caulfield III.

This was how it was. My father had been a mule.
He had flown down to Rio
Time and time again. But he courted disaster.
He tried to smuggle a wooden statue
Through the airport at Lima.
The Christ of the Andes. The statue was hollow.
He stumbled. It went and shattered.
And he had to stand idly by
As a cool fifty or sixty thousand dollars worth
Was trampled back into the good earth.

He would flee, to La Paz, then to Buenos Aires,
From alias to alias.
I imagined him sitting outside a hacienda
Somewhere in the Argentine.
He would peer for hours
Into the vastness of the pampas.
Or he might be pointing out the constellations
Of the Southern hemisphere
To the open-mouthed child at his elbow.
He sleeps with a loaded pistol under his pillow.

The mile-long white Cadillac had now wrapped
Itself round the Park Hotel.
We were spirited to the nineteenth floor
Where Caulfield located a secret door.
We climbed two perilous flights of steps
To the exclusive penthouse suite.
A moment later I was ushered
Into a chamber sealed with black drapes.
As I grew accustomed to the gloom
I realized there was someone else in the room.

He was huddled on an old orthopaedic mattress,
The makings of a skeleton,
Naked but for a pair of drawstring shorts.
His hair was waistlength, as was his beard.
He was covered in bedsores.
He raised one talon.
'I forgive you,' he croaked. 'And I forget.
On your way out, you tell that bastard
To bring me a dish of ice-cream.
I want Baskin-Robbins banana-nut ice-cream.'

I shimmied about the cavernous lobby.
Mr and Mrs Alfred Tennyson
Were ahead of me through the revolving door.
She tipped the bell-hop five dollars.
There was a steady stream of people
That flowed in one direction,
Faster and deeper,
That I would go along with, happily,
As I made my way back, like any other pilgrim,
To Main Street, to Foster's pool-room.

from
QUOOF

Gathering Mushrooms

The rain comes flapping through the yard
like a tablecloth that she hand-embroidered.
My mother has left it on the line.
It is sodden with rain.
The mushroom shed is windowless, wide,
its high-stacked wooden trays
hosed down with formaldehyde.
And my father has opened the Gates of Troy
to that first load of horse manure.
Barley straw. Gypsum. Dried blood. Ammonia.
Wagon after wagon
blusters in, a self-renewing gold-black dragon
we push to the back of the mind.
We have taken our pitchforks to the wind.

All brought back to me that September evening
fifteen years on. The pair of us
tripping through Barnett's fair demesne
like girls in long dresses
after a hail-storm.
We might have been thinking of the fire-bomb
that sent Malone House sky-high
and its priceless collection of linen
sky-high.
We might have wept with Elizabeth McCrum.
We were thinking only of psilocybin.
You sang of the maid you met on the dewy grass
And she stooped so low gave me to know
it was mushrooms she was gathering O.

He'll be wearing that same old donkey-jacket
and the sawn-off waders.
He carries a knife, two punnets, a bucket.
He reaches far into his own shadow.
We'll have taken him unawares
and stand behind him, slightly to one side.
He is one of those ancient warriors
before the rising tide.
He'll glance back from under his peaked cap
without breaking rhythm:
his coaxing a mushroom – a flat or a cup –
the nick against his right thumb;
the bucket then, the punnet to left or right,
and so on and so forth till kingdom come.

We followed the overgrown tow-path by the Lagan.
The sunset would deepen through cinnamon
to aubergine,
the wood-pigeon's concerto for oboe and strings,
allegro, blowing your mind.
And you were suddenly out of my ken, hurtling
towards the ever-receding ground,
into the maw
of a shimmering green-gold dragon.
You discovered yourself in some outbuilding
with your long-lost companion, me,
though my head had grown into the head of a horse
that shook its dirty-fair mane
and spoke this verse:

Come back to us. However cold and raw, your feet
were always meant
to negotiate terms with bare cement.
Beyond this concrete wall is a wall of concrete
and barbed wire. Your only hope
is to come back. If sing you must, let your song
tell of treading your own dung,
let straw and dung give a spring to your step.
If we never live to see the day we leap
into our true domain,
lie down with us now and wrap
yourself in the soiled grey blanket of Irish rain
that will, one day, bleach itself white.
Lie down with us and wait.

Trance

My mother opens the scullery door
on Christmas Eve, 1954,
to empty the dregs
of the tea-pot on the snowy flags.
A wind out of Siberia
carries such voices as will carry
through to the kitchen –

Someone mutters a flame from lichen
and eats the red-and white Fly Agaric
while the others hunker in the dark,
taking it in turn
to drink his mind-expanding urine.
One by one their reindeer
nuzzle in.

My mother slams the door
on her star-cluster of dregs
and packs me off to bed.
At 2 a.m. I will clamber downstairs
to glimpse the red-and-white
up the chimney, my new rocking-horse
as yet unsteady on its legs.

The Right Arm

I was three-ish
when I plunged my arm into the sweet-jar
for the last bit of clove-rock.

We kept a shop in Eglish
that sold bread, milk, butter, cheese,
bacon and eggs,
Andrews Liver Salts,
and, until now, clove-rock.

I would give my right arm to have known then
how Eglish was itself wedged between
ecclesia and *église*.

The Eglish sky was its own stained-glass vault
and my right arm was sleeved in glass
that has yet to shatter.

The Sightseers

My father and mother, my brother and sister
and I, with uncle Pat, our dour best-loved uncle,
had set out that Sunday afternoon in July
in his broken-down Ford

not to visit some graveyard – one died of shingles,
one of fever, another's knees turned to jelly –
but the brand-new roundabout at Ballygawley,
the first in mid-Ulster.

Uncle Pat was telling us how the B-Specials
had stopped him one night somewhere near Ballygawley
and smashed his bicycle

and made him sing the Sash and curse the Pope of Rome.
They held a pistol so hard against his forehead
there was still the mark of an O when he got home.

Quoof

How often have I carried our family word
for the hot water bottle
to a strange bed,
as my father would juggle a red-hot half-brick
in an old sock
to his childhood settle.
I have taken it into so many lovely heads
or laid it between us like a sword.

An hotel room in New York City
with a girl who spoke hardly any English,
my hand on her breast
like the smouldering one-off spoor of the yeti
or some other shy beast
that has yet to enter the language.

Glanders

When you happened to sprain your wrist or ankle
you made your way to the local shaman,
if 'shaman' is the word for Larry Toal,
who was so at ease with himself, so tranquil,

a cloud of smoke would graze on his thatch
like the cow in the cautionary tale,
while a tether of smoke curled down his chimney
and the end of the tether was attached

to Larry's ankle or to Larry's wrist.
He would conjure up a poultice of soot and spit
and flannel-talk, how he had a soft spot

for the mud of Flanders,
how he came within that of the cure for glanders
from a Suffolkman who suddenly went west.

Cherish the Ladies

In this, my last poem about my father,
there may be time enough
for him to fill their drinking-trough
and run his eye over

his three mooley heifers.
Such a well-worn path,
I know, from here to the galvanized bath.
I know, too, you would rather

I saw behind the hedge to where the pride
of the herd, though not an Irish
bull, would cherish
the ladies with his electric cattle-prod.

As it is, in my last poem about my father
he opens the stand-pipe
and the water scurries along the hose
till it's curled

in the bath. One heifer
may look up
and make a mental note, then put her nose
back to the salt-lick of the world.

Yggdrasill

From below, the waist-thick pine
seemed to arch
its back. It is a birch,
perhaps. At any rate, I could discern
a slight curvature of the spine.

They were gathered in knots
to watch me go.
A pony fouled the hard-packed snow
with her glib cairn,
someone opened a can of apricots.

As I climb
my nose is pressed to the bark.
The mark
of a cigarette burn
from your last night with him.

A snapshot of you and your sister
walking straight
through 1958,
The Works of Laurence Sterne
your only aid to posture.

The air is aerosol-
blue and chill. I have notched
up your pitch-
pine scent and the maidenhair fern's
spry arousal.

And it would be just swell and dandy
to answer
them with my tonsure,
to return
with the black page from *Tristram Shandy*.

Yet the lichened
tree trunk will taper
to a point where one scrap of paper
is spiked, and my people yearn
for a legend:

It may not be today
or tomorrow, but sooner or later
the Russians will water
their horses on the shores of Lough Erne
and Lough Neagh.

Mink

A mink escaped from a mink-farm
in South Armagh
is led to the grave of Robert Nairac
by the fur-lined hood of his anorak.

The Frog

Comes to mind as another small upheaval
amongst the rubble.
His eye matches exactly the bubble
in my spirit-level.
I set aside hammer and chisel
and take him on the trowel.

The entire population of Ireland
springs from a pair left to stand
overnight in a pond
in the gardens of Trinity College,
two bottles of wine left there to chill
after the Act of Union.

There is, surely, in this story
a moral. A moral for our times.
What if I put him to my head
and squeezed it out of him,
like the juice of freshly squeezed limes,
or a lemon sorbet?

Aisling

I was making my way home late one night
this summer, when I staggered
into a snow drift.

Her eyes spoke of a sloe-year,
her mouth a year of haws.

Was she Aurora, or the goddess Flora,
Artemidora, or Venus bright,
or Anorexia, who left
a lemon stain on my flannel sheet?

It's all much of a muchness.

In Belfast's Royal Victoria Hospital
a kidney machine
supports the latest hunger-striker
to have called off his fast, a saline
drip into his bag of brine.

A lick and a promise. Cuckoo spittle.
I hand my sample to Doctor Maw.
She gives me back a confident *All Clear*.

The More a Man Has the More a Man Wants

At four in the morning he wakes
to the yawn of brakes,
the snore of a diesel engine.
Gone. All she left
is a froth of bra and panties.
The scum of the Seine
and the Farset.
Gallogly squats in his own pelt.
A sodium street light
has brought a new dimension
to their black taxi.
By the time they force an entry
he'll have skedaddled
among hen runs and pigeon lofts.

The charter flight from Florida
touched down at Aldergrove
minutes earlier,
at 3.54 a.m.
Its excess baggage takes the form
of Mangas Jones, Esquire,
who is, as it turns out, Apache.
He carries only hand luggage.
'Anything to declare?'
He opens the powder-blue attaché-
case. 'A pebble of quartz.'
'You're an Apache?' 'Mescalero.'
He follows the corridor's
arroyo till the signs read *Hertz*.

He is going to put his foot down
on a patch of waste ground
along the Stranmillis embankment
when he gets wind
of their impromptu fire.
The air above the once-sweet stream
is aquarium-
drained.
And six, maybe seven, skinheads
have formed a quorum
round a burnt-out heavy-duty tyre.
So intent on sniffing glue
they may not notice Gallogly,
or, if they do, are so far gone.

Three miles west as the crow flies
an all-night carry-out
provides the cover
for an illegal drinking club.
While the bar man unpacks a crate
of Coca-Cola,
one cool customer
takes on all comers in a video game.
He grasps what his two acolytes
have failed to seize.
Don't they know what kind of take-away
this is, the glipes?
Vietmanese. Viet-ma-friggin'-*knees*.
He drops his payload of napalm.

Gallogly is wearing a candy-stripe
king-size sheet,
a little something he picked up
off a clothes line.
He is driving a milk van
he borrowed from the Belfast Co-op
while the milkman's back
was turned.
He had given the milkman a playful
rabbit punch.
When he stepped on the gas
he flooded the street
with broken glass.
He is trying to keep a low profile.

The unmarked police car draws level
with his last address.
A sergeant and eight constables
pile out of a tender
and hammer up the stairs.
The street bristles with static.
Their sniffer dog, a Labrador bitch,
bursts into the attic
like David Balfour in *Kidnapped*.
A constable on his first dawn swoop
leans on a shovel.
He has turned over a
new leaf in her ladyship's herb patch.
They'll take it back for analysis.

All a bit much after the night shift
to meet a milkman
who's double-parked his van
closing your front door after him.
He's sporting your
Donegal tweed suit and your
Sunday shoes and politely raises your
hat as he goes by.
You stand there with your mouth open
as he climbs into the still-warm
driving seat of your Cortina
and screeches off towards the motorway,
leaving you uncertain
of your still-warm wife's damp tuft.

Someone on their way to early Mass
will find her hog-tied
to the chapel gates –
O Child of Prague –
big-eyed, anorexic.
The lesson for today
is pinned to her bomber jacket.
It seems to read *Keep off the Grass*.
Her lovely head has been chopped
and changed.
For Beatrice, whose fathers
knew Louis Quinze,
to have come to this, her *perruque*
of tar and feathers.

He is pushing the maroon Cortina
through the sedge
on the banks of the Callan.
It took him a mere forty minutes
to skite up the M1.
He followed the exit sign
for Loughgall and hared
among the top-heavy apple orchards.
This stretch of the Armagh/Tyrone
border was planted by Warwickshiremen
who planted in turn
their familiar quick-set damson hedges.
The Cortina goes to the bottom.
Gallogly swallows a plummy-plum-plum.

'I'll warrant them's the very pair
o' boys I seen abroad
in McParland's bottom, though where
in under God –
for thou art so possessed with murd'rous hate –
where they come from God only knows.'
'They were mad for a bite o' mate,
I s'pose.'
'I doubt so. I come across a brave dale
o' half-chawed damsels. Wanst wun disappeared
I follied the wun as yelly as Indy male.'
'Ye weren't afeared?'
'I follied him.' 'God save us.'
'An' he driv away in a van belongin' t'*Avis*.'

The grass sprightly as Astroturf
in the September frost
and a mist
here where the ground is low.
He seizes his own wrist
as if, as if
Blind Pew again seized Jim
at the sign of the 'Admiral Benbow'.
As if Jim Hawkins led Blind Pew
to Billy Bones
and they were all one and the same,
he stares in disbelief
at an Aspirin-white spot he pressed
into his own palm.

Gallogly's thorn-proof tweed jacket
is now several sizes too big.
He has flopped
down in a hay shed
to ram a wad of hay into the toe
of each of his ill-fitting
brogues, when he gets the drift
of ham and eggs.
Now he's led by his own wet nose
to the hacienda-style
farmhouse, a baggy-kneed animated
bear drawn out of the woods
by an apple pie
left to cool on a windowsill.

She was standing at the picture window
with a glass of water
and a Valium
when she caught your man
in the reflection of her face.
He came
shaping past the milking parlour
as if he owned the place.
Such is the integrity
of their quarrel
that she immediately took down
the legally held shotgun
and let him have both barrels.
She had wanted only to clear the air.

Half a mile away across the valley
her husband's UDR patrol
is mounting a check-point.
He pricks up his ears
at the crack
of her prematurely arthritic hip-
joint,
and commandeers one of the jeeps.
There now, only a powder burn
as if her mascara had run.
The bloody puddle
in the yard, and the shilly-shally
of blood like a command wire
petering out behind a milk churn.

A hole in the heart, an ovarian
cyst.
Coming up the Bann
in a bubble.
Disappearing up his own bum.
Or, running on the spot
with all the minor aplomb
of a trick-cyclist.
So thin, side-on, you could spit
through him.
His six foot of pump water
bent double
in agony or laughter.
Keeping down-wind of everything.

White Annetts. Gillyflowers. Angel Bites.
When he names the forgotten names
of apples
he has them all off pat.
His eye like the eye of a travelling rat
lights on the studied negligence
of these scraws of turf.
A tarpaulin. A waterlogged pit.
He will take stock of the Kalashnikov's
filed-down serial number,
seven sticks of unstable
commercial gelignite
that have already begun to weep.
Red Strokes. Sugar Sweet. Widows Whelps.

Buy him a drink and he'll regale you
with how he came in for a cure
one morning after the night before
to the *Las Vegas* Lounge and Cabaret.
He was crossing the bar's
eternity of parquet floor
when his eagle eye
saw something move on the horizon.
If it wasn't an Indian.
A Sioux. An ugly Sioux.
He means, of course, an Oglala
Sioux busily tracing the family tree
of an Ulsterman who had some hand
in the massacre at Wounded Knee.

He will answer the hedge-sparrow's
Littlebitofbreadandnocheese
with a whole bunch
of freshly picked watercress,
a bulb of garlic,
sorrel,
with many-faceted blackberries.
Gallogly is out to lunch.
When his cock rattles its sabre
he takes it in his dab
hand, plants one chaste kiss
on its forelock,
and then, with a birl and a skirl,
tosses it off like a caber.

The UDR corporal had come off duty
to be with his wife
while the others set about
a follow-up search.
When he tramped out just before twelve
to exercise the greyhound
he was hit by a single high-velocity
shot.
You could, if you like, put your fist
in the exit wound
in his chest.
He slumps
in the spume of his own arterial blood
like an overturned paraffin lamp.

Gallogly lies down in the sheugh
to munch
through a Beauty of
Bath. He repeats himself, *Bath*,
under his garlic-breath.
Sheugh, he says. *Sheugh*.
He is finding that first 'sh'
increasingly difficult to manage.
Sh-leeps. A milkmaid sinks
her bare foot
to the ankle
in a simmering dung hill
and fills the slot
with beastlings for him to drink.

In Ovid's conspicuously tongue-in-cheek
account of an eyeball
to eyeball
between the goddess Leto
and a shower of Lycian reed cutters
who refuse her a cup of cloudy
water
from their churned-up lake,
Live then forever in that lake of yours,
she cries, and has them
bubble
and squeak
and plonk themselves down as bullfrogs
in their icy jissom.

A country man kneels on his cap
beside his neighbour's fresh
grave-mud
as Gallogly kneels to lap
the primrose-yellow
custard.
The knees of his hand-me-down duds
are gingerish.
A pernickety seven-
year-old girl-child
parades in her mother's trousseau
and mumbles a primrose
Kleenex tissue
to make sure her lipstick's even.

Gallogly has only to part the veil
of its stomach wall
to get right under the skin,
the spluttering heart
and collapsed lung,
of the horse in *Guernica*.
He flees the Museum of Modern Art
with its bit between his teeth.
When he began to cough
blood, Hamsun rode the Minneapolis/
New York night train
on top of the dining-car.
One long, inward howl.
A porter-drinker without a thrapple.

A weekend trip to the mountains
North of Boston
with Alice, Alice A.
and her paprika hair,
the ignition key
to her family's Winnebago camper,
her quim
biting the leg off her.
In the oyster bar
of Grand Central Station
she gobbles a dozen Chesapeakes –
'Oh, I'm not particular as to size' –
and, with a flourish of tabasco,
turns to gobble him.

A brewery lorry on a routine delivery
is taking a slow,
dangerous bend.
The driver's blethering
his code name
over the Citizens' Band
when someone ambles
in front of him. Go, Johnny, Go, Go, Go.
He's been dry-gulched
by a sixteen-year-old numb
with Mogadon,
whose face is masked by the seamless
black stocking filched
from his mum.

When who should walk in but Beatrice,
large as life, or larger,
sipping her one glass of lager
and singing her one song.
If he had it to do all over again
he would let her shave his head
in memory of '98
and her own, the French, Revolution.
The son of the King of the Moy
met this child on the Roxborough
estate. *Noblesse*, she said. *Noblesse
oblige.* And her tiny nipples
were bruise-bluish, wild raspberries.
The song she sang was 'The Croppy Boy'.

Her *grand'mère* was once asked to tea
by Gertrude Stein,
and her *grand'mère* and Gertrude
and Alice B., *chère* Alice B.
with her hook-nose,
the three of them sat in the nude
round the petits fours
and repeated *Eros is Eros is Eros.*
If he had it to do all over again
he would still be taken in
by her Alice B. Toklas
Nameless Cookies
and those new words she had him learn:
hash, hashish, *lo perfido assassin.*

Once the local councillor straps
himself into the safety belt
of his Citroën
and skids up the ramp
from the municipal car park
he upsets the delicate balance
of a mercury-tilt
boobytrap.
Once they collect his smithereens
he doesn't quite add up.
They're shy of a foot, and a calf
which stems
from his left shoe like a severely
pruned-back shrub.

Ten years before. The smooth-as-a-
front-lawn at Queen's
where she squats
before a psilocybin god.
The indomitable gentle-bush
that had Lanyon or Lynn
revise their elegant ground plan
for the university quad.
With calmness, with care,
with breast milk, with dew.
There's no cure now.
There's nothing left to do.
The mushrooms speak through her.
Hush-hush.

'Oh, I'm not particular as to size,'
Alice hastily replied
and broke off a bit of the edge
with each hand
and set to work very carefully,
nibbling
first at one
and then the other.
On the Staten Island Ferry
two men are dickering
over the price
of a shipment of Armalites,
as Henry Thoreau was wont to quibble
with Ralph Waldo Emerson.

That last night in the Algonquin
he met with a flurry
of sprites,
the assorted shades
of Wolfe Tone, Napper Tandy,
a sanguine
Michael Cusack
brandishing his blackthorn.
Then, Thomas Meagher
darts up from the Missouri
on a ray
of the morning star
to fiercely ask
what has become of Irish hurling.

Everyone has heard the story of
a strong and beautiful bug
which came out of the dry leaf
of an old table of apple-tree wood
that stood
in a farmer's kitchen in Massachusetts
and which was heard gnawing out
for several weeks –
When the phone trills
he is careful not to lose his page –
Who knows what beautiful and winged life
whose egg
has been buried for ages
may unexpectedly come forth? 'Tell-tale.

Gallogly carries a hunting bow
equipped
with a bow sight
and a quiver
of hunting arrows
belonging to her brother.
Alice has gone a little way off
to do her job.
A timber wolf,
a caribou,
or merely a trick of the light?
As, listlessly,
he lobs
an arrow into the undergrowth.

Had you followed the river Callan's
Pelorus Jack
through the worst drought
in living memory
to the rains of early Autumn
when it scrubs its swollen,
scab-encrusted back
under a bridge, the bridge you look down from,
you would be unlikely to pay much heed
to yet another old banger
no one could be bothered to tax,
or a beat-up fridge
well-stocked with gelignite,
or some five hundred yards of Cortex.

He lopes after the dribs of blood
through the pine forest
till they stop dead
in the ruins of a longhouse
or hogan.
Somehow, he finds his way
back to their tent.
Not so much as a whiff of her musk.
The girl behind the Aer Lingus
check-in desk
at Logan
is wearing the same scent
and an embroidered capital letter *A*
on her breast.

Was she Aurora, or the goddess Flora,
Artemidora, or Venus bright,
or Helen fair beyond compare
that Priam stole from the Grecian sight?
Quite modestly she answered me
and she gave her head one fetch up
and she said I am gathering musheroons
to make my mammy ketchup.
The dunt and dunder
of a culvert-bomb
wakes him
as it might have woke Leander.
And she said I am gathering musheroons
to make my mammy ketchup O.

Predictable as the gift of the gab
or a drop of the craythur
he noses round the six foot deep
crater.
Oblivious to their Landrover's
olive-drab
and the Burgundy berets
of a snatch-squad of Paratroopers.
Gallogly, or Gollogly,
otherwise known as Golightly,
otherwise known as Ingoldsby,
otherwise known as English,
gives forth one low cry of anguish
and agrees to come quietly.

They have bundled him into the cell
for a strip-
search.
He perches
on the balls of his toes, my my,
with his legs spread
till both his instep arches
fall.
He holds himself at arm's
length from the brilliantly Snowcem-ed
wall, a game bird
hung by its pinion tips
till it drops, in the fullness of time,
from the mast its colours are nailed to.

They have left him to cool his heels
after the obligatory
bath,
the mug shots, fingerprints
et cetera.
He plumps the thin bolster
and hints
at the slop bucket.
Six o'clock.
From the A Wing of Armagh jail
he can make out
the Angelus bell
of St Patrick's cathedral
and a chorus of 'For God and Ulster'.

The brewery lorry's stood at a list
by the *Las Vegas*
throughout the afternoon,
its off-side rear tyres down.
As yet, no one has looked agog
at the smuts and rusts
of a girlie mag
in disarray on the passenger seat.
An almost invisible, taut
fishing line
runs from the Playmate's navel
to a pivotal
beer keg.
As yet, no one has risen to the bait.

I saw no mountains, no enormous spaces,
no magical growth and metamorphosis
of buildings, nothing remotely like
a drama or a parable
in which he dons these lime-green
dungarees,
green Wellingtons,
a green helmet of aspect terrible.
The other world to which mescalin
admitted me was not the world of visions;
it existed out there, in what I could see
with my eyes open.
He straps a chemical pack on his back
and goes in search of some Gawain.

Gallogly pads along the block
to raise his visor
at the first peep-hole.
He shamelessly
takes in her lean piglet's
back, the back
and boyish hams
of a girl at stool.
At last. A tiny goat's-pill.
A stub of crayon
with which she has squiggled
a shamrock, yes,
but a shamrock after the school
of Pollock, Jackson Pollock.

I stopped and stared at her face to face
and on the spot a name came to me,
a name with a smooth, nervous sound:
Ylayali.
When she was very close
I drew myself up straight
and said in an impressive voice,
'Miss, you are losing your book.'
And Beatrice, for it is she, she squints
through the spy-hole
to pass him an orange,
an Outspan orange some visitor has spiked
with a syringe-ful
of vodka.

The more a man has the more a man wants,
the same I don't think true.
For I never met a man with one black eye
who ever wanted two.
In the *Las Vegas* Lounge and Cabaret
the resident group –
pot bellies, Aran knits –
have you eating out of their hands.
Never throw a brick at a drowning man
when you're near to a grocer's store.
Just throw him a cake of Sunlight soap,
let him wash himself ashore.
You will act the galoot, and gallivant,
and call for another encore.

Gallogly, Gallogly, O Gallogly
juggles
his name like an orange
between his outsize baseball glove
paws,
and ogles
a moon that's just out of range
beyond the perimeter wall.
He works a gobbet of Brylcreem
into his quiff
and delves
through sand and gravel,
shrugging it off
his velveteen shoulders and arms.

> *Just*
> *throw*
> *him*
> *a*
> *cake*
> *of*
> *Sunlight*
> *soap,*
> *let*
> *him*
> *wash*
> *him-*
> *self*
> *ashore.*

Into a picture by Edward Hopper
of a gas station
in the mid-West
where Hopper takes as his theme
light, the spooky
glow of an illuminated sign
reading Esso or Mobil
or what-have-you –
into such a desolate oval
ride two youths on a motorbike.
A hand gun. Balaclavas.
The pump attendant's grown so used
to hold-ups he calls after them:
Beannacht Dé ar an obair.

The pump attendant's not to know
he's being watched by a gallowglass
hot-foot from a woodcut
by Derricke,
who skips across the forecourt
and kicks the black
plastic bucket
they left as a memento.
Nor is the gallowglass any the wiser.
The bucket's packed with fertilizer
and a heady brew
of sugar and paraquat's
relentlessly gnawing its way through
the floppy knot of a Durex.

It was this self-same pump attendant
who dragged the head and torso
clear
and mouthed an Act of Contrition
in the frazzled ear
and overheard
those already-famous last words
Moose . . . Indian.
'Next of all wus the han'.' 'Be Japers.'
'The sodgers cordonned-off the area
wi' what-ye-may-call-it tape.'
'Lunimous.' 'They foun' this hairy
han' wi' a drowneded man's grip
on a lunimous stone no bigger than a . . .'

'Huh.'

from
MEETING THE BRITISH

Ontario

I spent last night in the nursery of a house in Pennsylvania. When I put out the light I made my way, barefoot, through the aftermath of Brandywine Creek. The constellations of the northern hemisphere were picked out in luminous paint on the ceiling. I lay under a comforting, phosphorescent Plough, thinking about where the Plough stopped being the Plough and became the Big Dipper. About the astronomer I met in Philadelphia who had found a star with a radio telescope. The star is now named after her, whatever her name happens to be. As all these stars grew dim, it seemed like a good time to rerun my own dream-visions. They had flashed up just as I got into bed on three successive nights in 1972. The first was a close-up of a face, Cox's face, falling. I heard next morning how he had come home drunk and taken a nose-dive down the stairs. Next, my uncle Pat's face, falling in slo-mo like the first, but bloody. It turned out he had slipped off a ladder on a building-site. His forehead needed seven stitches. Lastly, a freeze-frame trickle of water or glycerine on a sheet of smoked glass or perspex. I see it in shaving-mirrors. Dry martinis. Women's tears. On windshields. As planes take off or land. I remembered how I was meant to fly to Toronto this morning, to visit my younger brother. He used to be a research assistant at the University of Guelph, where he wrote a thesis on nitrogen-fixing in soya beans, or symbiosis, or some such mystery. He now works for the Corn Producers' Association of Ontario. On my last trip we went to a disco in the Park Plaza, where I helped a girl in a bin-liner dress to find her contact-lens.

—Did you know that Spinoza was a lens-grinder?

—Are you for real?

Joe was somewhere in the background, sniggering, flicking cosmic dandruff from his shoulders.

—A lens, I went on, is really a lentil. A pulse.

Her back was an imponderable, green furrow in the ultraviolet strobe.

—Did *you* know that Yonge Street's the longest street in the world?

—I can't say that I did.

—Well, it starts a thousand miles to the north, and it ends right here.

The Coney

Although I have never learned to mow
I suddenly found myself half-way through
last year's pea-sticks
and cauliflower-stalks
in our half-acre of garden.
My father had always left the whetstone
safely wrapped
in his old, tweed cap
and balanced on one particular plank
beside the septic tank.

This past winter he had been too ill
to work. The scythe would dull
so much more quickly in my hands
than his, and was so often honed,
that while the blade
grew less and less a blade
the whetstone had entirely disappeared
and a lop-eared
coney was now curled inside the cap.
He whistled to me through the gap

in his front teeth;
'I was wondering, chief,
if you happen to know the name
of the cauliflowers in your cold-frame
that you still hope to dibble
in this unenviable
bit of ground?'

'They would be *All the Year Round.*'
'I guessed as much'; with that he swaggered
along the diving-board

and jumped. The moment he hit the water
he lost his tattered
bathing-togs
to the swimming-pool's pack of dogs.
'Come in'; this flayed
coney would parade
and pirouette like honey on a spoon:
'Come on in, Paddy Muldoon.'
And although I have never learned to swim
I would willingly have followed him.

My Grandfather's Wake

If the houses in Wyeth's Christina's dream
and Malick's *Days of Heaven*
are triremes, yes,
triremes riding the 'sea of grain',
then each has a little barge
in tow—a freshly-dug grave.

I was trying to remember, Nancy,
how many New England graveyards you own,
all silver birch
and neat, white picket-fences.

If only that you might make room
for a nine-banded armadillo
found wandering in Meath
sometime in the 1860s;
a man-ox, a fish with three gold teeth
described by Giraldus Cambrensis.

Our cow chained in the byre
was a galley-slave from *Ben Hur*
to the old-fashioned child of seven
they had sent in search of a bucket of steam.

Profumo

My mother had slapped a month-long news embargo
on his very name. The inhalation
of my first, damp
menthol fag behind the Junior Common Room.

The violet-scented Thirteenth Birthday card
to which I would affix a stamp
with the Queen's head upside down, swalk,
and post to Frances Hagan.

The spontaneously-combustible *News of the World*
under my mother's cushion
as she shifted from ham to snobbish ham;

'Haven't I told you, time and time again,
that you and she are chalk
and cheese? Away and read Masefield's *Cargoes.'*

Chinook

I was micro-tagging Chinook salmon
on the Qu'Appelle
river.

I surged through the melt-water
in my crocus
waders.

I would give each brash,
cherubic
face its number.

Melt-water? These were sultry
Autumn
fish hang-gliding downstream.

Chinook. Their very name
a semantic
quibble.

The Autumn, then, of *Solidarity*,
your last in Cracow.
Your father

rising between borsch
and carp,
relinquishing the table to Pompeii.

The Wishbone

Maureen in England, Joseph in Guelph,
my mother in her grave.

  • • •

At three o'clock in the afternoon
we watch the Queen's
message to the Commonwealth
with the sound turned off.

  • • •

He seems to favour *Camelot*
over *To Have and Have Not*.

  • • •

Yet we agree, my father and myself,
that here is more than enough
for two; a frozen chicken,
spuds, sprouts, *Paxo* sage and onion.

  • • •

The wishbone like a rowelled spur
on the fibula of Sir ——— or Sir ———.

Meeting the British

We met the British in the dead of winter.
The sky was lavender

and the snow lavender-blue.
I could hear, far below,

the sound of two streams coming together
(both were frozen over)

and, no less strange,
myself calling out in French

across that forest-
clearing. Neither General Jeffrey Amherst

nor Colonel Henry Bouquet
could stomach our willow-tobacco.

As for the unusual
scent when the Colonel shook out his hand-

kerchief: *C'est la lavande,
une fleur mauve comme le ciel.*

They gave us six fishhooks
and two blankets embroidered with smallpox.

Christo's

Two workmen were carrying a sheet of asbestos
down the Main Street of Dingle;
it must have been nailed, at a slight angle,
to the same-sized gap between Brandon

and whichever's the next mountain.
Nine o'clock. We watched the village dogs
take turns to spritz the hotel's refuse-sacks.
I remembered Tralee's unbiodegradable flags

from the time of the hunger-strikes.
We drove all day past mounds of sugar-beet,
hay-stacks, silage-pits, building-sites,
a thatched cottage even—

all of them draped in black polythene
and weighted against the north-east wind
by concrete blocks, old tyres; bags of sand
at a makeshift army post

across the border. By the time we got to Belfast
the whole of Ireland would be under wraps
like, as I said, 'one of your man's landscapes'.
'Your man's? You don't mean Christo's?'

The Fox

Such an alarm
as was raised last night
by the geese
on John Mackle's goose-farm.

I got up and opened
the Venetian blind.
You lay
three fields away

in Collegelands
graveyard, in ground
so wet you weren't so much
buried there as drowned.

That was a month ago.
I see your face
above its bib
pumped full of formaldehyde.

You seem engrossed,
as if I'd come on you
painfully writing your name
with a carpenter's pencil

on the lid
of a mushroom-box.
You're saying, *Go back to bed.*
It's only yon dog-fox.

The Soap-Pig

I must have been dozing in the tub
when the telephone
rang and a small, white grub
crawled along the line
and into my head:
Michael Heffernan was dead.

All I could think of
was his Christmas present
from what must have been 1975.
It squatted there on the wash-stand,
an amber, pig-shaped
bar of soap.

He had breezed into Belfast
in a three-quarter length coney-fur
to take up the post
of Drama Producer
with the still-reputable Beeb,
where I had somehow wangled a job.

Together we learned from Denys
Hawthorne and Allan McClelland
to float, like Saint Gennys,
on our own hands
through airwaves mostly jammed by cub-
reporters and poisoned pups.

He liked to listen at full tilt
to bootleg tapes

of Ian Paisley's assaults
on Papes,
regretful only that they weren't in quad.
His favourite word was *quidditas*.

I could just see the jesuitical,
kitsch-camp slip-
knot in the tail
of even that bar of soap.
For this was Heffernan
saying, 'You stink to high heaven.'

Which I well knew. Many's an Arts Club
night with Barfield and Mason
ended with me throwing up
at the basin.
Anne-Marie looked on, her unspoken,
'That's to wash, not boke in.'

This, or any, form of self-regard
cut no ice
with Michael, who'd undergone heart-
surgery at least twice
while I knew him. On a trip
once to the Wexford slobs

he and I had shared
a hotel room. When he slipped
off his shirt
there were two unfashionably-broad lap-
els where the surgeons had sawn
through the xylophone

on which he liked to play
Chopin or *Chop*
sticks until he was blue
in the face; be-bop, doo-wop:
they'd given him a tiny, plastic valve
that would, it seemed, no more dissolve

than the soap-pig I carried
on successive flits
from Marlborough Park (and Anne-
Marie)
to the Malone Avenue flat
(*Chez Moy*, it was later dubbed)
to the rented house in Dub (as in *Dub-*

lin) Lane,
until, at last, in Landseer Street
Mary unpeeled its cellophane
and it landed on its feet
among porcelain, glass and heliotrope
pigs from all parts of the globe.

When we went on holiday to France
our house-sitter was troub-
led by an unearthly fragrance
at one particular step
on the landing. It was no pooka,
of course, but the camomile soap-pig

that Mary, in a fit of pique,
would later fling into the back yard.
As I unpicked

the anthracite-shards
from its body, I glimpsed the scrab-
nosed, condemned slab

of our sow that dropped
dead from a chill in 1966,
its uneven litter individually wrapped
in a banana box
with polystyrene and wood-shavings;
this time Mary was leaving,

taking with her the gold
and silver pigs, the ivory.
For Michael Heffernan, the common cold
was an uncommon worry
that might as easily have stopped
him in his tracks. He'd long since escaped

Belfast for London's dog-eat-dog
back-stab
and leap-frog.
More than once he collap-
sed at his desk. But Margaret
would steady him through the Secretariat

towards their favourite restaurant
where, given my natural funk
I think of as restraint,
I might have avoided that Irish drunk
whose slow jibes
Michael parried, but whose quick jab

left him forever at a loss for words.
For how he would delib-
erate on whether two six-foot boards
sealed with ship's
varnish and two tea-chests
(another move) on which all this rests

is a table; or this merely a token
of some ur-chair,
or—being broken—
a chair at all: the mind's a razor
on the body's strop.
And the soap-pig? It's a bar of soap,

now the soap-sliver
in a flowered dish
that I work each morning into a lather
with my father's wobbling-brush,
then reconcile to its pool of glop
on my mother's wash-stand's marble top.

Sushi

'Why do we waste so much time in arguing?'
We were sitting at the sushi-bar
drinking *Kirin* beer
and watching the Master chef
fastidiously shave
salmon, tuna and yellowtail
while a slightly more volatile
apprentice
fanned the rice,
every grain of which was magnetised
in one direction—east.
Then came translucent strips
of octopus,
squid and conger,
pickled ginger
and pale-green horseradish . . .
'It's as if you've some kind of death-wish.
You won't even talk . . .'
On the sidewalk
a woman in a leotard
with a real leopard
in tow.
For an instant I saw beyond the roe
of sea-urchins,
the erogenous
zones of shad and sea-bream;
I saw, when the steam
cleared, how this apprentice
had scrimshandered a rose's

exquisite petals
not from some precious metal
or wood or stone
('I might just as well be eating alone.')
but the tail-end of a carrot:
how when he submitted this work of art
to the Master—
Is it not the height of arrogance
to propose that God's no more arcane
than the smack of oregano,
orgone,
the inner organs
of beasts and fowls, the mines of Arigna,
the poems of Louis Aragon?—
it might have been alabaster
or jade
the Master so gravely weighed
from hand to hand
with the look of a man unlikely to confound
Duns Scotus, say, with Scotus Eriugena.

7, Middagh Street

Wystan

Quinquereme of Nineveh from distant Ophir;
a blizzard off the Newfoundland coast
had, as we slept, metamorphosed

the *Champlain*'s decks
to a wedding cake,
on whose uppermost tier stood Christopher

and I like a diminutive bride and groom.
A heavy-skirted Liberty would lunge
with her ice-cream
at two small, anxious

boys, and Erika so grimly wave
from the quarantine-launch
she might as truly have been my wife
as, later that day, Barcelona was Franco's.

• • •

There was a time when I thought it mattered
what happened in Madrid

or Seville
and, in a sense, I haven't changed
my mind; the forces of Good and Evil
were indeed ranged

against each other, though not unambiguously.
I went there on the off-chance
they'd let me try
my hand at driving an ambulance;

there turned out to be some bureau-
cratic hitch.
When I set out for the front on a black burro
it promptly threw me in the ditch.

I lay there for a year, disillusioned, dirty,
until a firing-party

of Chinese soldiers
came by, leading dishevelled ponies.
They arranged a few sedimentary boulders
over the body of a Japanese

spy they'd shot
but weren't inclined to bury,
so that one of his feet stuck out.
When a brindled pariah

began to gnaw
on it, I recognised the markings of the pup
whose abscessed paw
my father had lanced on our limestone doorstep.

        · · ·

Those crucial years he tended
the British wounded

in Egypt, Gallipoli
and France, I learned to play

Isolde to my mother's Tristan.
Are they now tempted to rechristen

their youngest son
who turned his back on Albion

a Quisling?
Would their chaise-longue

philosophers have me somehow inflate
myself and float

above their factories and pylons
like a flat-footed barrage-balloon?

. . .

For though I would gladly return to Eden
as that ambulance-driver
or air-raid warden
I will never again ford the river
to parley with the mugwumps
and fob them off with monocles and mumps;
I will not go back as *Auden*.

. . .

And were Yeats living at this hour
it should be in some ruined tower

not malachited Ballylee
where he paid out to those below

one gilt-edged scroll from his pencil
as though he were part-Rapunzel

and partly Delphic oracle.
As for his crass, rhetorical

posturing, 'Did that play of mine
send out certain men (*certain* men?)

the English shot . . . ?'
the answer is 'Certainly not'.

If Yeats had saved his pencil-lead
would certain men have stayed in bed?

For history's a twisted root
with art its small, translucent fruit

and never the other way round.
The roots by which we were once bound

are severed here, in any case,
and we are all now dispossessed;

prince, poet, construction worker,
salesman, soda fountain jerker—

all equally isolated.
Each loads flour, sugar and salted

beef into a covered wagon
and strikes out for his Oregon,

each straining for the ghostly axe
of a huge, blond-haired lumberjack.

. . .

'If you want me look for me under your boot-soles';
When I visited him in a New Hampshire hospital
where he had almost gone for a Burton
with peritonitis
Louis propped himself up on an ottoman
and read aloud the ode to Whitman
from *Poeta en Nueva York.*
The impossible Eleanor Clark
had smuggled in a pail of oysters and clams
and a fifth column
of Armagnac.
Carson McCullers extemporised a blues harmonica
of urinous pipkins and pannikins
that would have flummoxed Benjamin Franklin.
I left them, so, to the reign
of the ear of corn
and the journey-work of the grass-leaf
and found my way next morning to Bread Loaf
and the diamond-shaped clearing in the forest
where I learned to play softball with Robert Frost.

. . .

For I have leapt with Kierkegaard
out of the realm of Brunel and Arkwright

with its mills, canals and railway-bridges
into this great void
where Chester and I exchanged love-pledges
and vowed

our marriage-vows. As he lay asleep
last night the bronze of his exposed left leg
made me want nothing so much as to weep.
I thought of the terrier, of plague,

of Aschenbach at the Lido.
Here was my historical
Mr W.H., my 'onlie begetter' and fair lady;
for nothing this wide universe I call . . .

Gypsy

Save thou, my rose; in it thou art my all.
In Mother's dream my sister, June,
was dressed in her usual cal-
ico but whistling an unfamiliar tune
when a needlecord
dea ex machina
came hoofing it across the boards—
a Texan moo-cow
with a red flannel tongue,
a Madamish leer
and a way with the song
it insinuated into Mother's ear;
'You've only to put me in the act
to be sure of the Orpheum contract.'

She did. We followed that corduroy cow
through Michigan, Kansas,
Idaho.
But the vaudeville audiences
were dwindling. Mack Sennett's
Bathing Beauties
had seen to that. Shakespeare's Sonnets,
Das Kapital, Boethius,
Dainty June and her Newsboy Songsters—
all would succumb to Prohibition,

G-men, gangsters,
bathtub gin.
June went legit. In Minneapolis
I spirit-gummed pink gauze on my nipples.

And suddenly I was waiting in the wings
for the big production-routine
to end. I was wearing a swanky
gaberdine
over my costume of sherbet-green tulle.
I watched two girl-Pawnees
in little else but pony-tails
ride two paint ponies
on a carousel. They loosed mock arrows
into the crowd, then hung
on for dear life when the first five rows
were showered with horse-dung.
I've rarely felt so close to nature
as in Billy Minsky's Burlesque Theatre.

This was Brooklyn, 1931. I was an under-age
sixteen. Abbott and Costello
were sent out front while the stage
was hosed down and the ponies hustled
back to the Ben Hur stables.
By the time I came on
the customers were standing on the tables,
snapping like caymans
and booing even the fancy cyclorama
depicting the garden of Eden.
Gradually the clamour
faded as I shed

all but three of my green taffeta fig-leaves
and stood naked as Eve.

'I loved the act. Maybe you'd wannah buy
Sam?' asked Nudina, over a drink.
Nudina danced with a boa
constrictor that lived under the sink
in the women's room. 'He's a dear.'
'So *this* is a speakeasy,'
Mother whispered. We'd ordered beer
and pizza.
'Don't look now,' said Nudina, 'but Waxey's
just come in.' 'Waxey?' 'A friend of mine
from Jersey. Runs applejack
through special pipelines
in the sewers. Never even been subpoenaed.
But let's get back to discussing the serpent.'

I've no time for any of that unladylike stuff.
An off-the-shoulder shoulder-strap,
the removal of one glove—
it's knowing exactly when to stop
that matters,
what to hold back, some sweet disorder . . .
The same goes for the world of letters.
When I met George Davis in Detroit
he managed the Seven Arts
bookstore. I was on the Orpheum circuit.
Never, he says, give all thy heart;
there's more enterprise in walking not quite
naked. Now he has me confined to quarters
while we try to solve *The G-String Murders*.

We were looking over my scrapbook entries
from *The New Yorker*,
Fortune, Town & Country,
when I came on this from the *Daily Worker*;
'Striptease is a capitalistic cancer,
a product of the profit system.'
Perhaps we cannot tell the dancer
from the dance. Though I've grown accustomed
to returning the stare
of a life-size cut-out of Gypsy Rose Lee
from the World's Fair
or the Ziegfeld Follies
I keep that papier-mâché cow's head packed
just in case vaudeville does come back.

Ben

Come back, Peter. Come back, Ben Britten.
The monstrous baritone

of a flushed, ungainly
Cyril Connolly

swaggers across the ocean
from the crow's-nest of *Horizon*

to chide Pimpernell and Parsnip
with deserting Europe's 'sinking ship';

Auden and Isherwood
have no sense of the greater good

but 'an eye on the main chance'.
Harold Nicolson's latest intelligence

has them in league with Goebbels.
And the Dean of St Paul's?—

'Since you left us, the stink is less.'
Then a question in the House.

The Minister, in his reply, takes Wystan
for the tennis-star H. W. Austin

which, given his line in tennis shoes
(though not the soup-stained ties

and refusal ever to change his smalls)
seems just. Perhaps the Dean of St Paul's

himself did time
with Uncle Wizz in an airless room

(a collaboration on *John* Bunyan?)
and has some grounds for his opinion.

In this, as in so many things,
it won't be over till the fat lady sings.

Chester

The fat lady sings to Der Rosenkavalier
Die Zeit, die ist ein sonderbar Ding;

in time Octavian will leave her
for Sophie, Sophie

leave Ochs:
Feldmarschalls trade their Marschallins
for those time-honoured trophies—
cunts, or fresh, young cocks.

Among the miscellaneous
Jack Tars
I met last week in a Sands Street bar

I came on one whose uncircumcised dong's
sand-vein was a seam of beryl, abstruse
as this lobster's.

Salvador

This lobster's not a lobster but the telephone
that rang for Neville Chamberlain.

It droops from a bare branch
above a plate, on which the remains of lunch

include a snapshot of Hitler
and some boiled beans left over

from *Soft Construction: A Premonition
of Civil War*. When Breton

hauled me before his kangaroo-court
I quoted the Manifesto; we must disregard

moral and aesthetic considerations
for the integrity of our dream-visions.

What if I dreamed of Hitler as a masochist
who raises his fist

only to be beaten?
I might have dreamed of fucking André Breton

he so pooh-poohed my *Enigma of William Tell.*
There I have Lenin kneel

with one massive elongated buttock
and the elongated peak

of his cap supported by two forked sticks.
This time there's a raw beef-steak

on the son's head. My father croons a lullaby.
Is it that to refer, however obliquely,

is to refer? In October, 1934,
I left Barcelona by the back door

with a portfolio of work
for my first one-man show in New York.

A starry night. The howling of dogs.
The Anarchist taxi-driver carried two flags,

Spanish and Catalan. Which side was I on?
Not one, or both, or none.

I who had knelt with Lenin in Breton's court
and sworn allegiance to the proletariat

had seen the chasm
between myself and Surrealism

begin as a hair-crack on a tile.
In *Soft Construction* I painted a giant troll

tearing itself apart limb
by outlandish limb.

Among the broken statues of Valladolid
there's one whose foot's still welded

to the granite plinth
from which, like us, it draws its strength.

From that, and from those few boiled beans.
We cannot gormandise upon

the flesh of Cain and Abel
without some melancholic vegetable

bringing us back to earth, to the boudoir
in the abattoir.

Our civil wars, the crumbling of empires,
the starry nights without number

safely under our belts,
have only slightly modified the tilt

of the acanthus leaf,
its spiky puce-and-alabaster an end in itself.

Carson

In itself, this old, three-storey brownstone
is unremarkable, and yet so vivid was the reverie
in which it appeared to George one night
that when he drove
next morning to Brooklyn Heights
he found it true. I had just left Reeves
and needed a place to stay. As must Wynstan,

dear Wynnie-Pooh, who's given to caution
the rest of us every
time we sit down, be it to jerky
or this afternoon's Thanksgiving dinner, every
blessed time, 'We'll have crawfish, turkey,
salad and savoury,
and no political discussion'—

a form of grace
that would surely have raised an eyebrow
at even the Last Supper,
never mind a household where no time ago
when the Richard Wrights moved in the super

moved out, unwilling, it seemed, to draw and hew
and tend the furnace for fellow Negroes.

Nothing is too much bother
for Eva, our cook, a former Cotton Club chorine
whom Gypsy found, who can so glamourise
pork-belly, grits and greens
I imagine myself back in Columbus,
Georgia, imagine, indeed a paddle-steamer careen
and clarion up the East River

from the Chattahoochee, its cargo of blue dimity,
oil lamps and the things
of childhood washed
overboard; my Christmas stocking
limps from the stern like an oriole's nest:
when an orange in the toe spreads its black wing
the stocking, too, is empty.

The magnolia tree at my window's a bonsai
in the glass globe
I jiggle like a cocktail-
waiter from the Keynote Club,
so that Chester's Kwakiutl
false-face and glib,
Jane and Paul Bowles, the chimpanzee

and its trainer, Gypsy
and hers, are briefly caught up in an eddy
of snow; pennies
from heaven, Wynstan's *odi*
atque amo of Seconal and bennies:

then my cloudy
globe unclouds to reveal the tipsy

MacNeice a monarch
lying in state on a Steinway baby grand
between the rotting
carcasses of two pack-mules from *Un Chien Andalou*
while a strait-laced Benjamin Britten
picks out a rondo
in some elusive minor key.

If only I might as readily dismiss
the chord a fire-siren struck
in all of us this afternoon (we chased the engines
two or three blocks
till we tired) or the ingenuous
slow-slow-quick
I felt again for Reeves—the Dismas

on my right side—or Erika Mann's
piercing my left
as we stood in Cranberry Street; flute-music,
panting of hinds, her spindrift
gaze; peacocks, sandalwood, the musky
otto of her cleft:
two girls, I thought, two girls in silk kimonos.

Louis

Both beautiful, one a gazebo.
When Hart Crane fell
from the *Orizaba*
it was into the *trou normand* of the well

at Carrickfergus castle.
All very Ovidian,
as the ghostly
Healfdene

once remarked of both sorts of kipper
we were forced to eat
at supper

every night in Reykjavik;
one tasted of toe-nails, one of the thick
skin on the soles of the feet.

             •   •   •

He now affects an ulster lined with coypu
and sashays like an albino rabbit
down the same Fifth Avenue
where Avida Dollars
once squired an ocelot
on a solid

gold chain snaffled from Bonwit Teller's.
It seems that Scott Fitzgerald wrote *Ivanhoe*
or the *Rubàiyàt*
and Chester Kallman = Agape.

. . .

Wystan likes to tell how he lost his faith
in human nature

in a movie-theatre
at 85th

and York, where the neighbourhood Huns
had taken a break from baking buns

to egg
on Hitler to his *Sieg*

im Poland; the heavy bear that went to bed
with Delmore Schwartz was bad

and the rye in Yorkville's *Schwartzbrot*
shot through with ergot.

Since when he's set himself up as a stylite
waiting for hostilities

to cease, a Dutch master
intent only on painting an oyster

or lemon
(all those afternoons in the Ashmolean)

or the slur of light in a red goblet
while Montagues and Capulets

run riot, as they did five years ago
in the Short Strand and Sandy Row.

Then my father preached 'Forget the past'
and episcopised

into the wind
and again refused to sign the Covenant;

though the seam of gold a Unitedman strikes
in Wicklow in 1796

which Parnell will later pan and assay
to make a ring for Kitty O'Shea

was well and truly played
out, no bishop could ever quite contemplate

a life merely nasty, British and short.
Delmore was ushered

from that same movie-theatre
with 'Everything you do matters';

the displacement of soap-suds in a basin
may have some repercussion

for a distant ship:
only last night I tried to butt the uneven

pages of a *Belfast Newsletter* from 1937
into some sort of shape . . .

.   .   .

Imagine a great white highway
a quarter of a mile broad
extending the length of Ireland
from the Giant's Causeway
to Mizen Head
and you can grasp the magnitude
of our annual output of linen.

.   .   .

Among the blue flowers of the flax a linnet
sang out 'Lundy'

at the implications of that bleach-
green. 'It was merely a figure of speech.'

'Call it what you like.
The grey skies of an Irish Republic

are as nothing compared to this blue dome.'
He tailed off over the flax-dam

to return with a charm of goldfinches
who assailed me with their 'Not an inch'

and their 'No', and yet again, 'No'.
As they asperged me with kerosene

I recognised the voice of Sir Edward Carson;
'Bid me strike a match and blow.'

. . .

In dreams begin responsibilities;
it was on account of just such an allegory
that Lorca
was riddled with bullets

and lay mouth-down
in the fickle shadow of his own blood.
As the drunken soldiers of the *Gypsy Ballads*
started back for town

they heard him calling through the mist,
'When I die leave the balcony shutters open.'
For poetry *can* make things happen—
not only can, but *must*—

and the very painting of that oyster
is in itself a political gesture.

As O'Daly well knows. It was in the olive-grove
where Lorca's buried
that he envisaged *Two Pieces of Bread
Expressing the Idea of Love*

with its miniature duellists and chess-pawn
expressing also his idea of Spain.
(If only he were here
today to make his meaning absolutely clear.)

' So that, for me, brandy and smoked
quail and crumpled baguette
conjure O'Daly, then themselves, then Beckett's
'¡Uptherepublic!',

then Beatrice and Benedick
in the back seat of Eleanor's mother's Pontiac.

.   .   .

After drinking all night in a Sands Street shebeen
where a sailor played a melodeon
made from a merman's spine
I left by the back door of Muldoon's

(it might have been the Rotterdam)
on a Monday morning, falling in with
the thousands of shipyardmen who tramped
towards the front gates of Harland and Wolff.

The one-eyed foreman had strayed out of Homer.
'MacNeice? That's a Fenian name.'
As if to say, 'None of your sort, none of you

will as much as go for a rubber hammer
never mind chalk a rivet, never mind caulk a seam
on the quinquereme of Nineveh.'